Who Needs These Services?

-STUDENTS

-CLERGY

-NON-PROFIT ORGANIZATIONS

-NEIGHBORHOOD COMMUNITY GROUPS

-PUBLIC OFFICIALS

-BLOCK CLUBS

-FRATERNITIES AND SORORITIES

A Comprehensive Guide to Community Development

Phillip Sims, Author

Contents

Introduction

"A well planned and executed project becomes its own engine and thus propels itself."

By the end of this workshop, participants will be able to:

- Serve their community
- Receive a step-by-step guide through the development of community
- Build a functional, accomplished, and lasting community

Introduction

This handbook is intended to serve community leaders, neighborhoods, students, and volunteers as a step-by-step guide through the development of community projects. You will find information on how to prepare and lead communities in the revitalization of their neighborhood with the use of local resources.

Designed from real-life experiences, the following steps will assist readers in their efforts to build a functional, accomplished and lasting community, and additionally help everyone understand that no matter the size of their contribution, their involvement matters to achieve an overall improved quality of life.

"A well planned and executed project becomes its own engine and thus propels itself."

Step One

Develop Your Team

- What are you looking towards?
- What will it take?
- Who will it take?

Develop Your Board of Directors

Establishing a Board of Directors is important before you begin any community development project and organization. The Board defines the direction that the organization will be working towards. They also help with various types of research, including initial analysis of demographics being served and funding sources. When selecting your Board, you should choose individuals that have a proven history of skills necessary to effectively propel your mission.

Board members are considered valuable to any organization because they are influential people in their community. It is important to select positive, excited, and motivated individuals, because their energy towards building a safe and prosperous neighborhood will influence others in and outside the community.

Make sure your supporters are strong and reliable leaders with a clear understanding of the purpose and goals of the organization. Having a defined mission and vision statement are very important to have, because they will serve as a guide.

The Chairperson, Vice Chairperson, Secretary and Treasurer should be the first positions selected. You are building from the ground up and these specific volunteer roles are vital during the planning and preparation stages.

Define board member roles before they take office so everyone is aware of their tasks and responsibilities from the start. An example of board responsibilities are as follows:

Chairperson

- Works close with volunteered and board to ensure all projects are on time and on budget.
- Open, lead, and close all board and emergency meetings.
- Responsible for encouragement of volunteers, community

- outreach, and relations.
- Communicate directly with Vice Chairperson, Treasurer, Secretary and all other acting officers.

Vice Chairperson

- In absence of Chairperson, the Vice Chairperson assumes the responsibilities of the chairperson.
- Works closely with board volunteers and community during and beyond the development process.
- Encourage volunteerism through community outreach.

Secretary

- Must be fluent in technology.
- Required to keep accurate minutes of all meetings.
- Records the proceedings of all meetings.
- Calls meetings to order in absence of the Chairperson and Vice Chairperson.
- Communicates organization updates and notices to other members of the board.
- Encourages the participation and works closely with volunteers and community to develop activities for the community.

Treasurer

- Keeps accurate account of all monies and donations.
- Prepares proper documents necessary for funding.
- Encourages volunteers to participate in community outreach and activities.
- Facilitates meetings in absence of Chairperson, Vice Chairperson, and Secretary.

Parliamentarian

- Keeps meeting on target and on time.
- Serves as meeting moderator.
- Knowledgeable of bylaws and ensures board acts in accordance with rules and regulations.

It is also important to mention that your established board is now essentially a corporation and is subject to liabilities (sexual harassment, misconduct, lawsuit, and accidents on company business and time). Purchase insurance and complete background checks on each board member. If a volunteer commits a crime while acting on behalf of the organization, the company can be sued.

Lastly, during the development of your board establish a set of by-laws. By-laws are a set of rules your directors are governed by, which you can build upon as your project grows. An example of by-laws can be found below:

ABC 123 CORPORATION

TABLE OF CONTENTS
ORGANIZATION BYLAWS

BYLAWS OF ABC 123 CORPORATION

ARTICLE I

This organization shall be called **ABC 123 Corporation** (the "A1C"), known herein as ORG.

ARTICLE II PURPOSE

ORG is organized as a non-profit, non-stock, directorship community development corporation. As a development corporation, the mission of ORG shall be to strengthen educational, economic and cultural opportunities to improve the quality of life for City and surrounding communities. To operate exclusively for the purpose set forth in Section 501© (3) of the Revenue Service Code of 1986, as amended (the "Code"), including for such purposes the making of contributions to organizations that qualify as exempt organizations under the Code.

After a Board has been established, regular meetings are important and encouraged to keep early volunteers, stakeholders and supporters engaged and updated on the progress of the project and to build team morale. Make sure to keep all meetings on target with established topics and goals. Volunteers should leave each meeting with an action items, goals, and resources to attain their goal.

These meetings will also be essential for communicating safety information, generating awareness, and can serve as a platform to celebrate successes and milestones.

Additional Tip: Invite locale police departments, council members, and other area officials to speak at your organization's monthly meetings. They are good resources to call for information as well as implement and support change in the neighborhood.

Step Two

Incorporate Your Corporation

- Your purpose?
- Your name?
- What type of business?
- Forms to incorporate business.

Incorporate Your Corporation

With the goal of finding a name suitable for your purpose, remember you will be using this name on marketing materials, business cards, and anything business related moving forward. Before you become too attached to a name, utilize the many resources available online and in state office to make sure your desired name isn't already in use. After you confirm your name is not already in use, contact your attorney to get the necessary forms to incorporate a business name, which will include documenting the purpose of the corporation.

A document that you will need to file is a 501©(3)*(1), a collaboration of federal forms needed for your corporation to be considered tax deductible. People will be more open to giving if their donations are tax deductible, especially to major corporation.

Additional Tip:

Have an accountant with 501©(3) experience complete the necessary form. It can be very time consuming to complete. A 501©(3) typically takes about four to six months to be approved.

CSCL/CD-502 (Rev. 10/17)

MICHIGAN DEPARTMENT OF LICENSING AND REGULATORY AFFAIRS
CORPORATIONS, SECURITIES & COMMERCIAL LICENSING BUREAU

Date Received	AC1
	This document is effective on the date filed, unless a subsequent effective date within 90 days after received date is stated in the document.

Name		
Person who will sign		
Address		
Address of business		
City	State	ZIP Code
City,	State, 12345	

EFFECTIVE DATE:

Document will be returned to the name and address you enter above.
If left blank, document will be returned to the registered office.

ARTICLES OF INCORPORATION
For use by Domestic Nonprofit Corporations
(Please read information and instructions on the last page)

Pursuant to the provisions of Act 162, Public Acts of 1982, the undersigned corporation executes the following Articles:

ARTICLE I

The name of the corporation is:

ABC 123 Corporation

ARTICLE II

The purpose or purposes for which the corporation is formed are:
To engage in educational, charitable and scientific purposes under the meaning of 501(c)(3) U.S. Internal Revenue Code to purchase, own, and operate housing space which is to be rented below market value rates.

ARTICLE III

1. The corporation is formed upon a Nonstock basis.
(Stock or Nonstock)

2. If formed on a stock basis, the total number of shares the corporation has authority to issue is ________. If the shares are or are to be divided into classes, the designation of each class, the number of shares in each class, and the relative rights, preferences and limitations of the shares of each class to the extent that the designations, numbers, relative rights, preferences, and limitations have been determined are as follows:

Form **1023**

(Rev. December 2017)
Department of the Treasury
Internal Revenue Service

Application for Recognition of Exemption Under Section 501(c)(3) of the Internal Revenue Code

▶ **Do not enter social security numbers on this form as it may be made public.**
▶ **Go to *www.irs.gov/Form1023* for instructions and the latest information.**

OMB No. 1545-0056

Note: If exempt status is approved, this application will be open for public inspection.

*Use the instructions to complete this application and for a definition of all **bold** items.* For additional help, call IRS Exempt Organizations Customer Account Services toll-free at 1-877-829-5500. Visit our website at ***www.irs.gov*** for forms and publications. If the required information and documents are not submitted with payment of the appropriate user fee, the application may be returned to you.

Attach additional sheets to this application if you need more space to answer fully. Put your name and EIN on each sheet and identify each answer by Part and line number. Complete Parts I – XI of Form 1023 and submit only those Schedules (A through H) that apply to you.

Part I Identification of Applicant

1 Full name of organization (exactly as it appears in your **organizing document**)		2 c/o Name (if applicable)	
ABC123CORPORATION		A1C	
3 **Mailing address** (Number and street) (see instructions)	Room/Suite	4 Employer Identification Number (EIN)	
12345 Address St.		12-3456789	
City or town, state or country, and ZIP + 4		5 Month the annual accounting period ends (01 – 12)	
City, State 12345-6789		12	
6 Primary contact (officer, director, trustee, or **authorized representative**) a Name: President		b Phone: (123) 456-7890	
		c Fax: (optional)	
7 Are you represented by an authorized representative, such as an attorney or accountant? If "Yes," provide the authorized representative's name, and the name and address of the authorized representative's firm. Include a completed Form 2848, *Power of Attorney and Declaration of Representative*, with your application if you would like us to communicate with your representative.		☐ Yes	☑ No
8 Was a person who is not one of your officers, directors, trustees, employees, or an authorized representative listed in line 7, paid, or promised payment, to help plan, manage, or advise you about the structure or activities of your organization, or about your financial or tax matters? If "Yes," provide the person's name, the name and address of the person's firm, the amounts paid or promised to be paid, and describe that person's role.		☐ Yes	☑ No
9a Organization's website: A1C.org			
b Organization's email: (optional)			
10 Certain organizations are not required to file an information return (Form 990 or Form 990-EZ). If you are granted tax-exemption, are you claiming to be excused from filing Form 990 or Form 990-EZ? If "Yes," explain. See the instructions for a description of organizations not required to file Form 990 or Form 990-EZ.		☐ Yes	☑ No
11 Date incorporated if a corporation, or formed, if other than a corporation. (MM/DD/YYYY)		MM / DD / YYYY	
12 Were you formed under the laws of a **foreign country**? If "Yes," state the country.		☐ Yes	☑ No

For Paperwork Reduction Act Notice, see instructions. Cat. No. 17133K Form **1023** (Rev. 12-2017)

Form **8718**

(Rev. March 2018)

Department of the Treasury
Internal Revenue Service

User Fee for Exempt Organization Determination Letter Request

▶ **Attach this form to determination letter application.**
(Form 8718 is NOT a determination letter application.)
▶ **Go to *www.irs.gov/Form8718* for the latest information.**

OMB No. 1545-1798

For IRS Use Only — Control number ______ Amount paid ______ User fee screener ______

Name of organization	Employer Identification Number
ABC 123 CORPORATION	12-3456789

Caution: Do not attach Form 8718 to an application for a pension plan determination letter. Use Form 8717 instead.

1 **Type of request**	**Fee**
a ☑ Application for recognition of exemption under section 501 or under section 521 from organizations (other than pension, profit-sharing, and stock bonus plans described in section 401). Enter the applicable fee amount . . . . ▶ $	3000.00
b ☐ Group exemption letters . . . . ▶ $	

Section references are to the Internal Revenue Code, unless otherwise noted.

Instructions

The law requires payment of a user fee with each application for a determination letter. For more information, see Rev. Proc. 2018-5, 2018-1 I.R.B. 233, or latest annual update, available on IRS.gov.

Check only one box on line 1 for the type of application you are submitting. Then, enter the appropriate user fee amount in the space provided.

Caution: The application will not be processed without payment of the proper user fee.

Attach to Form 8718 a check or money order payable to the "United States Treasury" for the full amount of the user fee. If you do not include the full amount, your application will be returned. Attach Form 8718 to your determination letter application.

Generally, the user fee will be refunded only if the Internal Revenue Service declines to issue a determination.

Where To File

Send the determination letter application and Form 8718 to:

Internal Revenue Service
P.O. Box 12192
Covington, KY 41012-0192

Who Should File

Organizations applying for federal income tax exemption, other than filers of Form 1023, Application for Recognition of Exemption Under Section 501(c)(3), or Form 1023-EZ (filed only electronically), should file Form 8718.

Paperwork Reduction Act Notice. We ask for the information on this form to carry out the Internal Revenue laws of the United States. If you want your organization to be recognized as tax-exempt by the IRS, you are required to give us this information. We need it to determine whether the organization meets the legal requirements for tax-exempt status.

You are not required to provide the information requested on a form that is subject to the Paperwork Reduction Act unless the form displays a valid OMB control number. Books or records relating to a form or its instructions must be retained as long as their contents may become material in the administration of any Internal Revenue law. The rules governing the confidentiality of Form 8718 are covered in section 6104.

The time needed to complete and file this form will vary depending on individual circumstances. The estimated average time is 5 minutes. If you have suggestions for making this form simpler, we would be happy to hear from you. You can send us comments from *IRS.gov/FormComments*. Or you can send your comments to the Internal Revenue Service, Tax Forms and Publications, 1111 Constitution Ave. NW, IR-6526, Washington, DC 20224. Do not send the form to this address. Instead, see *Where To File*, above.

Cat. No. 64728Z — Form **8718** (Rev. 3-2018)

Step Three

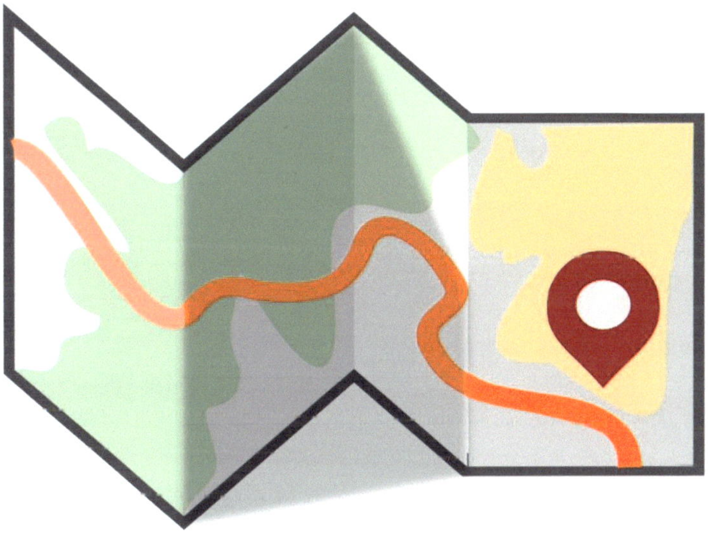

Establish a Location

- Location… Location... LOCATION!
- How to create a clean and safe community.
- What do the people want?
- Get the neighborhood involved.

Establish a Location

Congratulations, you've made it to chapter 3, which means you're well on your way to starting your community development project!

Location is essential to the success of your project. It is always a good idea to survey the area of choice by interviewing neighborhood residents to evaluate and address their needs. During these conversations, you may find a few people who are resistant to change. Unfortunately, every resident in the neighborhood of your choice may not be enthusiastic about your development plans. Recognize those people and work to gain their consensus by remaining transparent about your goals and intentions while addressing their concerns.

You should also be familiar with your neighborhood of choice. This can be done through helpful initiatives like bi-annual cleaning days. Every neighborhood, no matter the condition, can benefit from a regular cleaning. Start one and make it fun! This event can also be in conjunction with your local city governments clean up days. Take the initiative a step further by taking inventory of all the vacant and dilapidated property and use your County Registry of Deeds to find ownership information to encourage maintenance or selling the property.

The location of your project can also help to bring in more funding. Many companies will invest quicker in areas that are up and coming rather than completely decrepit areas.

Here are some additional and important tips to consider when choosing a location:

- Old gas station sites and manufacturing plants are extremely difficult to develop. They are environmental hazards that often require the removal of underground storage tanks and toxic wastes, which can very expensive. Note: The government could possibly have "Brownfield Dollars" * (2) to assist in the removal.
- Tire dump sites are costly to clean up and it is quite

problematic to dispose of that type of material.

- Closed school buildings may have a great amount of asbestos and lead paint in them. The cost for the cleanup can usually be expensive. However, this is another instance where the "Brownfield Dollars" from the state or federal government may be available to help in clean up.

Creating a clean and safe community

If you took a survey to assess the most important attribute(s) of great a neighborhood, a majority of people will emphasize that safety is most important, followed by cleanliness. Everyone desires and deserves to live in a clean and safe neighborhood.

You may be surprised with how many people would love to get involved in-group efforts to beautify the neighborhood. Use available resources to make this undertaking as proficient as possible. For example, when I was starting a community development organization, I used interns from the University of

Michigan to fill in a map of existing houses and properties in a nine-block radius. Each property's condition was documented, whether it was as simple as cutting a lawn or fixing a window to as grand as needing to tear down the entire structure. We were able to save time and money while still assessing the needs of the community.

In the same project, I sought out the non-profit organization called "the Community Legal Resource," who performs title searches for all necessary legal actions to acquire said property.

Additional Tip: If an owner of vacant and dilapidated property refuses to make repairs to get the property up to standards and chooses not to demolish the property, it would be a wise investment to contact your City or County Government Nuisance and Abatement Department concerning the safety of the residents and they will handle the situation accordingly. If the vacant properties are in good shape, they can be rehabbed and incorporated into your project. However, don't fall victim to accepting "free" land. Although it may seem like the perfect opportunity, there are many unforeseen problems with these properties and land.

Step Four
Create a Site Plan

- What is a site plan?
- Who should be involved?

Create a site plan

A site plan is a detailed architectural landscape plan of proposed improvements and most commonly shows a building footprint, parking, lighting, and other landscaping elements. The site plan is a simulation of your vision. Be sure to seek out input from the neighborhood to incorporate into your plan. If you do not communicate with your community, you risk uproar and rejection of your project.

After you have your plan laid out on paper, work with a design student, professional architect or designer to create a three-dimensional layout of the proposed plan. This will give everyone an idea of exactly what you are planning and see the possibilities for the proposed area.

At the very core, site plans are necessary to acquire funding, a site plan shows how serious you are about your project. Potential sponsors, city and state officials are less likely to respond to your development project without a site plan. A lack of a site plan is seen as a lack of vision.

Additional Tip: In your site plan for community development projects, you must know what zoning area your project will be functioning. Here is a breakdown of Zoning Terms:

R1 – Single Family Residential District
Single Family Detached Homes

R2 – Two Family Residential District
Single family detached and attached homes and two-family homes (up to 2 families living in a multi-unit).

R3 – Medium Density Residential District
A range of single-family to multi-family homes. Many uses are available for this zone, more community apartment structures.

Step Five

Acquire Community Stakeholders

- Get familiar with people.
- Who to contact?
- Create relationships.

Acquire Community Stakeholders

A stakeholder is a person or group that has an investment, share or interest in your project. A stakeholder must see the benefit of the project in order for them to participate. Acquiring community partnerships and stakeholder that reflect the interest and values of your community project is a must.

The role of partnerships and stakeholders in regard to community development is to bring resources, functionality, expertise and credibility to the project. Creating a partnership with local hospitals, churches, schools and businesses is essential to the success of your community development project. Your organization can also solicit students to help volunteer on numerous projects within your program.

Young people love to get involved in organizations with positive and fun initiatives. Let these volunteers use their creativity to support outreach efforts and communicate your organization's goals through brochures, fliers, monthly newsletters, speaking engagements and social media.

Additional Tip: Before soliciting services, check your state's requirements for Soliciting Licenses. You do not want to get fined for unlawful soliciting.

Step Six

Perform Market Analysis

- Know your area
- What is needed and why?

Market Analysis is a documented study and investigation of current conditions. The goals of the study are to determine the appropriateness of your project and the possibility of its success in that particular area. An analysis of the area will help determine the community's needs and ultimately help you understand if it's a good decision to start your proposed community project.

A market study is taking your research one step further as a way to get the community involved in your analysis. It's essentially an interview of individuals in the neighborhood to assess what is necessary for your organization to achieve success.

The most helpful tools to start with in the assessment of an area are the Census Tracts and Block Numbers Areas. These components give insight on the race, age, and other basic demographics of the people in your area.

See example of a Census Consumer Expenditures Report.

U.S. Census Bureau

AMERICAN FactFinder

DP05 | ACS Demographic and Housing Estimates: 2006-2008

2006-2008 American Community Survey 3-Year Estimates

For information on confidentiality protection, sampling error, nonsampling error, and definitions, see Survey Methodology.

Geography: United States

ACS Demographic and Housing Estimates	Number		Percent	
	Estimate	Margin of Error	Estimate	Margin of Error
SEX AND AGE				
Total population	301,237,703	*****	301,237,703	(X)
Male	148,418,500	+/-11,524	49.3%	+/-0.1
Female	152,819,203	+/-11,528	50.7%	+/-0.1
Under 5 years	20,672,826	+/-7,730	6.9%	+/-0.1
5 to 9 years	19,773,981	+/-26,612	6.6%	+/-0.1
10 to 14 years	20,425,884	+/-26,319	6.8%	+/-0.1
15 to 19 years	21,650,392	+/-15,332	7.2%	+/-0.1
20 to 24 years	20,920,044	+/-15,370	6.9%	+/-0.1
25 to 34 years	40,125,972	+/-14,231	13.3%	+/-0.1
35 to 44 years	43,140,679	+/-12,910	14.3%	+/-0.1
45 to 54 years	43,865,767	+/-11,521	14.6%	+/-0.1
55 to 59 years	18,210,745	+/-28,353	6.0%	+/-0.1
60 to 64 years	14,471,277	+/-27,550	4.8%	+/-0.1
65 to 74 years	19,488,145	+/-6,488	6.5%	+/-0.1
75 to 84 years	13,313,618	+/-18,960	4.4%	+/-0.1
85 years and over	5,178,373	+/-18,347	1.7%	+/-0.1
Median age (years)	36.7	+/-0.1	(X)	(X)
18 years and over	227,431,128	+/-13,385	75.5%	+/-0.1
21 years and over	214,184,670	+/-35,577	71.1%	+/-0.1
62 years and over	46,025,037	+/-19,248	15.3%	+/-0.1
65 years and over	37,980,136	+/-7,120	12.6%	+/-0.1
18 years and over	227,431,128	+/-13,385	227,431,128	(X)
Male	110,641,970	+/-10,621	48.6%	+/-0.1
Female	116,789,158	+/-9,779	51.4%	+/-0.1
65 years and over	37,980,136	+/-7,120	37,980,136	(X)
Male	16,008,865	+/-4,220	42.2%	+/-0.1
Female	21,971,271	+/-4,849	57.8%	+/-0.1
RACE				
Total population	301,237,703	*****	301,237,703	(X)
One race	294,665,998	+/-45,274	97.8%	+/-0.1
Two or more races	6,571,705	+/-45,246	2.2%	+/-0.1
One race	294,665,998	+/-45,274	97.8%	+/-0.1
White	223,965,009	+/-63,750	74.3%	+/-0.1
Black or African American	37,131,771	+/-28,694	12.3%	+/-0.1
American Indian and Alaska Native	2,419,895	+/-14,633	0.8%	+/-0.1
Cherokee tribal grouping	284,519	+/-5,724	0.1%	+/-0.1
Chippewa tribal grouping	107,791	+/-3,200	0.0%	+/-0.1
Navajo tribal grouping	296,669	+/-6,234	0.1%	+/-0.1
Sioux tribal grouping	114,174	+/-3,174	0.0%	+/-0.1
Asian	13,164,169	+/-17,493	4.4%	+/-0.1
Asian Indian	2,503,921	+/-25,495	0.8%	+/-0.1

ACS Demographic and Housing Estimates	Number		Percent	
	Estimate	Margin of Error	Estimate	Margin of Error
Chinese	3,051,605	+/-23,776	1.0%	+/-0.1
Filipino	2,366,501	+/-21,504	0.8%	+/-0.1
Japanese	776,640	+/-9,777	0.3%	+/-0.1
Korean	1,329,342	+/-14,363	0.4%	+/-0.1
Vietnamese	1,464,611	+/-20,208	0.5%	+/-0.1
Other Asian	1,671,549	+/-20,643	0.6%	+/-0.1
Native Hawaiian and Other Pacific Islander	446,164	+/-6,518	0.1%	+/-0.1
Native Hawaiian	150,899	+/-5,480	0.1%	+/-0.1
Guamanian or Chamorro	76,515	+/-4,806	0.0%	+/-0.1
Samoan	73,407	+/-5,118	0.0%	+/-0.1
Other Pacific Islander	145,343	+/-5,283	0.0%	+/-0.1
Some other race	17,538,990	+/-58,473	5.8%	+/-0.1
Two or more races	6,571,705	+/-45,246	2.2%	+/-0.1
White and Black or African American	1,461,491	+/-18,147	0.5%	+/-0.1
White and American Indian and Alaska Native	1,530,793	+/-11,781	0.5%	+/-0.1
White and Asian	1,099,412	+/-14,857	0.4%	+/-0.1
Black or African American and American Indian and Alaska Native	259,469	+/-8,150	0.1%	+/-0.1
Race alone or in combination with one or more other races				
Total population	301,237,703	*****	301,237,703	(X)
White	229,600,160	+/-70,329	76.2%	+/-0.1
Black or African American	39,477,170	+/-23,154	13.1%	+/-0.1
American Indian and Alaska Native	4,560,735	+/-10,827	1.5%	+/-0.1
Asian	14,863,151	+/-14,008	4.9%	+/-0.1
Native Hawaiian and Other Pacific Islander	845,713	+/-8,251	0.3%	+/-0.1
Some other race	18,972,069	+/-60,361	6.3%	+/-0.1
HISPANIC OR LATINO AND RACE				
Total population	301,237,703	*****	301,237,703	(X)
Hispanic or Latino (of any race)	45,432,158	+/-5,828	15.1%	+/-0.1
Mexican	29,318,971	+/-52,779	9.7%	+/-0.1
Puerto Rican	4,127,728	+/-28,732	1.4%	+/-0.1
Cuban	1,572,138	+/-15,633	0.5%	+/-0.1
Other Hispanic or Latino	10,413,321	+/-47,852	3.5%	+/-0.1
Not Hispanic or Latino	255,805,545	+/-5,825	84.9%	+/-0.1
White alone	198,420,355	+/-10,793	65.9%	+/-0.1
Black or African American alone	36,397,922	+/-23,532	12.1%	+/-0.1
American Indian and Alaska Native alone	2,041,269	+/-11,520	0.7%	+/-0.1
Asian alone	13,000,306	+/-16,990	4.3%	+/-0.1
Native Hawaiian and Other Pacific Islander alone	413,294	+/-5,340	0.1%	+/-0.1
Some other race alone	737,938	+/-12,595	0.2%	+/-0.1
Two or more races	4,794,461	+/-30,020	1.6%	+/-0.1
Two races including Some other race	228,452	+/-6,757	0.1%	+/-0.1
Two races excluding Some other race, and Three or more races	4,566,009	+/-28,888	1.5%	+/-0.1
Total housing units	127,762,925	+/-5,291	(X)	(X)

Data are based on a sample and are subject to sampling variability. The degree of uncertainty for an estimate arising from sampling variability is represented through the use of a margin of error. The value shown here is the 90 percent margin of error. The margin of error can be interpreted roughly as providing a 90 percent probability that the interval defined by the estimate minus the margin of error and the estimate plus the margin of error (the lower and upper confidence bounds) contains the true value. In addition to sampling variability, the ACS estimates are subject to nonsampling error (for a discussion of nonsampling variability, see Accuracy of the Data). The effect of nonsampling error is not represented in these tables.

Notes:

While the 2008 American Community Survey (ACS) data generally reflect the November 2007 Office of Management and Budget (OMB) definitions of metropolitan and micropolitan statistical areas; in certain instances the names, codes, and boundaries of the principal cities shown in ACS tables may differ from the OMB definitions due to differences in the effective dates of the geographic entities. The 2008 Puerto Rico Community Survey (PRCS) data generally reflect the November 2007 Office of Management and Budget (OMB) definitions of metropolitan and micropolitan statistical areas; in certain instances the names, codes, and boundaries of the principal cities shown in PRCS tables may differ from the OMB definitions due to differences in the effective dates of the geographic entities.

Estimates of urban and rural population, housing units, and characteristics reflect boundaries of urban areas defined based on Census 2000 data. Boundaries for urban areas have not been updated since Census 2000. As a result, data for urban and rural areas from the ACS do not necessarily reflect the results of ongoing urbanization.

Explanation of Symbols:
1. An '**' entry in the margin of error column indicates that either no sample observations or too few sample observations were available to compute a standard error and thus the margin of error. A statistical test is not appropriate.
2. An '-' entry in the estimate column indicates that either no sample observations or too few sample observations were available to compute an estimate, or a ratio of medians cannot be calculated because one or both of the median estimates falls in the lowest interval or upper interval of an open-ended distribution.
3. An '-' following a median estimate means the median falls in the lowest interval of an open-ended distribution.
4. An '+' following a median estimate means the median falls in the upper interval of an open-ended distribution.
5. An '***' entry in the margin of error column indicates that the median falls in the lowest interval or upper interval of an open-ended distribution. A statistical test is not appropriate.
6. An '*****' entry in the margin of error column indicates that the estimate is controlled. A statistical test for sampling variability is not appropriate.

Source: U.S. Census Bureau, 2006-2008 American Community Survey

ACS Demographic and Housing Estimates	Number		Percent	
	Estimate	Margin of Error	Estimate	Margin of Error
Chinese	3,051,605	+/-23,776	1.0%	+/-0.1
Filipino	2,366,501	+/-21,504	0.8%	+/-0.1
Japanese	776,640	+/-9,777	0.3%	+/-0.1
Korean	1,329,342	+/-14,363	0.4%	+/-0.1
Vietnamese	1,464,611	+/-20,208	0.5%	+/-0.1
Other Asian	1,671,549	+/-20,643	0.6%	+/-0.1
Native Hawaiian and Other Pacific Islander	446,164	+/-6,518	0.1%	+/-0.1
Native Hawaiian	150,899	+/-5,480	0.1%	+/-0.1
Guamanian or Chamorro	76,515	+/-4,806	0.0%	+/-0.1
Samoan	73,407	+/-5,118	0.0%	+/-0.1
Other Pacific Islander	145,343	+/-5,283	0.0%	+/-0.1
Some other race	17,538,990	+/-58,473	5.8%	+/-0.1
Two or more races	6,571,705	+/-45,246	2.2%	+/-0.1
White and Black or African American	1,461,491	+/-18,147	0.5%	+/-0.1
White and American Indian and Alaska Native	1,530,793	+/-11,781	0.5%	+/-0.1
White and Asian	1,099,412	+/-14,857	0.4%	+/-0.1
Black or African American and American Indian and Alaska Native	259,469	+/-8,150	0.1%	+/-0.1
Race alone or in combination with one or more other races				
Total population	301,237,703	*****	301,237,703	(X)
White	229,600,160	+/-70,329	76.2%	+/-0.1
Black or African American	39,477,170	+/-23,154	13.1%	+/-0.1
American Indian and Alaska Native	4,560,735	+/-19,827	1.5%	+/-0.1
Asian	14,863,151	+/-14,008	4.9%	+/-0.1
Native Hawaiian and Other Pacific Islander	845,713	+/-8,251	0.3%	+/-0.1
Some other race	18,972,069	+/-60,361	6.3%	+/-0.1
HISPANIC OR LATINO AND RACE				
Total population	301,237,703	*****	301,237,703	(X)
Hispanic or Latino (of any race)	45,432,158	+/-5,828	15.1%	+/-0.1
Mexican	29,318,971	+/-52,779	9.7%	+/-0.1
Puerto Rican	4,127,728	+/-28,732	1.4%	+/-0.1
Cuban	1,572,138	+/-15,633	0.5%	+/-0.1
Other Hispanic or Latino	10,413,321	+/-47,852	3.5%	+/-0.1
Not Hispanic or Latino	255,805,545	+/-5,825	84.9%	+/-0.1
White alone	198,420,355	+/-10,793	65.9%	+/-0.1
Black or African American alone	36,397,922	+/-23,532	12.1%	+/-0.1
American Indian and Alaska Native alone	2,041,269	+/-11,520	0.7%	+/-0.1
Asian alone	13,000,306	+/-16,990	4.3%	+/-0.1
Native Hawaiian and Other Pacific Islander alone	413,294	+/-5,340	0.1%	+/-0.1
Some other race alone	737,938	+/-12,595	0.2%	+/-0.1
Two or more races	4,794,461	+/-30,020	1.6%	+/-0.1
Two races including Some other race	228,452	+/-6,757	0.1%	+/-0.1
Two races excluding Some other race, and Three or more races	4,566,009	+/-28,888	1.5%	+/-0.1
Total housing units	127,762,925	+/-5,291	(X)	(X)

Data are based on a sample and are subject to sampling variability. The degree of uncertainty for an estimate arising from sampling variability is represented through the use of a margin of error. The value shown here is the 90 percent margin of error. The margin of error can be interpreted roughly as providing a 90 percent probability that the interval defined by the estimate minus the margin of error and the estimate plus the margin of error (the lower and upper confidence bounds) contains the true value. In addition to sampling variability, the ACS estimates are subject to nonsampling error (for a discussion of nonsampling variability, see Accuracy of the Data). The effect of nonsampling error is not represented in these tables.

Notes:

While the 2008 American Community Survey (ACS) data generally reflect the November 2007 Office of Management and Budget (OMB) definitions of metropolitan and micropolitan statistical areas; in certain instances the names, codes, and boundaries of the principal cities shown in ACS tables may differ from the OMB definitions due to differences in the effective dates of the geographic entities. The 2008 Puerto Rico Community Survey (PRCS) data generally reflect the November 2007 Office of Management and Budget (OMB) definitions of metropolitan and micropolitan statistical areas; in certain instances the names, codes, and boundaries of the principal cities shown in PRCS tables may differ from the OMB definitions due to differences in the effective dates of the geographic entities.

Estimates of urban and rural population, housing units, and characteristics reflect boundaries of urban areas defined based on Census 2000 data. Boundaries for urban areas have not been updated since Census 2000. As a result, data for urban and rural areas from the ACS do not necessarily reflect the results of ongoing urbanization.

Explanation of Symbols:
1. An '**' entry in the margin of error column indicates that either no sample observations or too few sample observations were available to compute a standard error and thus the margin of error. A statistical test is not appropriate.
2. An '-' entry in the estimate column indicates that either no sample observations or too few sample observations were available to compute an estimate, or a ratio of medians cannot be calculated because one or both of the median estimates falls in the lowest interval or upper interval of an open-ended distribution.
3. An '-' following a median estimate means the median falls in the lowest interval of an open-ended distribution.
4. An '+' following a median estimate means the median falls in the upper interval of an open-ended distribution.
5. An '***' entry in the margin of error column indicates that the median falls in the lowest interval or upper interval of an open-ended distribution. A statistical test is not appropriate.
6. An '*****' entry in the margin of error column indicates that the estimate is controlled. A statistical test for sampling variability is not appropriate.

Source: U.S. Census Bureau, 2006-2008 American Community Survey

Step Seven

Establish a Budget

- What is a budget?
- Why is it needed?
- Count the cost.
- What will it take?

Establish a Budget

With all businesses, establishing a budget is a must. This is where your treasurer will be most efficient.

It is the treasurer's job to have a good idea of all expected costs, which will determine how much funding is necessary for each stage of the development process. There are quite a few items necessary to include in a budget. Researching and identifying cost is vitally important to the stability and continuation of your project. A budget will also make it easier to show investors and the community exactly where and what their money is being used for.

Additionally, make sure a contingency plan is also a part of your overall budget. It is impossible to know all of the cost associated with building a project, no matter how extensive the research. A budget must include funding for contingencies and unforeseen circumstances.

Additional Tip: If you are asking for donations, make those a part of your budget. At this stage, you should have already acquired a 501©(3) status if you are a non-profit. The budget is not only for money going, but for money coming in as well. Set a donations goal for your budget and project.

On the next page you will find an example preliminary budget.

Pre-Development Budget

Marketing	$1,500
Legal	$1,500
Legal Filing Fees	$2,000
Accounting	$1,000
Printing/Flyers/Advertisement	$700
Strategic Plan	$10,000
Office Personnel	$5,000
Executive Director	$20,000
Administrative Assistant	$10,000
Office Rent	$12,000
Office Supplies	$2,000
Good Faith Offer	$5,000
Total	$72,700

Step Eight

Acquire Funding

- How to pay for the cost
- What to look for
- Where to get the funds

Acquire Funding

There is funding available to community initiatives on all levels, whether it be governmental, federal, state, or local. Although in the last couple of years, funding has slowed down, there are still many resources and steps you can take to acquire financial assistance.

First, it is important to know that there are two types of funding that can be obtained: predevelopment and development. Predevelopment funds are used for the planning stages, including the market analysis, development of site plans, consulting and other steps discussed in previous chapters. Good predevelopment resources can be corporate sponsorship, for example, funding from banks, insurance companies, sports teams, local colleges and universities. Foundation and community grants and the Neighborhood Opportunity

Fund (NOF), as well as recognizing Local Initiatives Support Corporation (LISC) (which is a national organization committed to helping cities restore communities by supporting many causes), are also all great additional resources.

Development funds are used for the actual construction of your project and can come from municipality planning and development programs such as Home Fund, Community Level Block Grants (CDBC), Low Income Housing Tax Credit (LIHTC), and New Market Tax Credit (NMTC). You can also contact your state's office of development for grant opportunities.

Lastly, partnership and collaborations with other groups are also excellent ways to receive funding. A for-profit development can partner with a non-profit developer, which results in advantages for both groups. The non-profit can get monies that a for-profit cannot, and in some cases, the for-profit company has the business expertise that a non-profit does not.

Here are a few examples of the types of funding necessary:

Types of Funding

Public Funds

1. Federal Agencies
   a. Organizations not individuals typically apply for public funding depending on the type of grant
      i. Institutions for Higher Education
      ii. Local government agencies
      iii. Non-profits organizations
      iv. Hospitals
   b. In order to apply for Federal funding an Organization must have
      i. 501 © 3
      ii. DUNS number call (866)-705-5711 to obtain a number.
   c. There are two types of Federal Grants
      i. Competitive – is based on the best suitor for the grant.
      ii. Non-Competitive is like open grant funding.

2. Government
   a. Federal Grant Websites*
      i. Websites for federal agencies (allows access to open grants available. Example: www.grants.gov)
      ii. Search engine
      iii. RSS feeds

3. County, & Municipal
   a. County & Municipal Websites
      i. Website for county agencies. (Allows access to open grants available. Example: www.waynecounty.gov)
      ii. County and local government create their own processes for funding programs and projects.

Private Funds

1. Foundations
    a. Awards to Private or Non-profit tax exempt (Humane Society)
        i. General Support
        ii. Endowment
        iii. Program or Project Grants
        iv. Matching or Challenge Grants
        v. Fellowship/Scholarships

2. Corporation
    a. Professional & Trade Associations
        i. Direct giving
        ii. Donations
        iii. Advertising/Sponsorship
        iv. Fundraising Activities

3. Foundations
    a. Family (William Ford)
    b. Corporate (Ford Motor Company)
    c. Community (Kresge Center in Michigan)
    d. Industry – Related (DTE Energy)

4. Corporation (including Financial Institutions)
    a. Grant / In-Kind donation (Volunteers of America)
    b. WIIFM (what is in it for me) Factor (Target)

5. Local Organization
    a. Service Organization (LISC – Local Initiative Service Corporation)
    b. Public Charities (United Way)
    c. Interest Groups (Labor Union)
    d. Fraternities/Sororities (Zeta Phi Beta Sorority, Inc.)

the conclusion.

Conclusion

- Closing Tips

Conclusion

(Let's get started!!)

Having an impactful and sustainable development is possible. In order to successfully achieve this goal, you will need a great development team, which must include:

Developer(s) – The person(s) responsible for many tasks, such as land purchasing and becoming familiar with zoning issues, financing issues, environmental issues

Architect – The person(s) responsible for site plans, construction management and building documents.

Accountant – The person(s) responsible for filing necessary documents for funding and keeping your organization in good standing with the federal, state, and local government.

Contractor – The person(s) responsible for keeping construction on plan and budget. Analyzing bid contracts, scheduling, managing expectations and keeping projects in compliance with building codes.

Attorney – The person or team responsible for organizing and reviewing all legal documents necessary for all steps of the project. They should provide legal advice whenever necessary and assist in the closing of all contracts. Your attorney should have experience in Federal and State programs and regulations, county and city laws and provide assistances in acquiring all the necessary documents to successfully develop your project.

city laws and provide assistances in acquiring all the necessary documents to successfully develop your project.

Every one of these members, in addition to your governing Board are vitally important to the overall progress and success of your project – yourself included!

Success is possible by following the steps that have been outlined in this quick guide. And remember, there are many public sources available to assist you at every step, for any development project you choose to undertake.

Closing Tips

- Always represent yourself as a professional. Use a letterhead for all correspondences and any form of business-related writing. Also remember that everyone you come in contact with during and after the development of your project is a potential investor or beneficial contact. You and your board members should have business cards on hand at all times to distribute when making and establishing contacts.
- Never underestimate the power of social media as a way to connect with not only your immediate community, but also the entire world. Utilize modern technology in efforts to improve the community. For example, Facebook and Instagram and excellent platforms to share how you are impacting the community through status updates and photos. Twitter is also a useful tool for keeping the community regularly updated in short and simple.

VALUABLE
DEVELOPEMENT
SOLUTIONS
www.valuabledevelopmentsolutions.com

"Everybody Has A Value"

Who I Am

Phil Sims; an expert Community Economic Development Consultant. My experience was gained over twenty-three (23) years of hands on, direct involvement in every facet of construction, project development, project management, i.e., budgeting, funding, and organizing stakeholders and benefactors. My most significant project was with my own church and its surrounding community. The geography of the project is more than 4 square miles and benefited more than 20% of the total community population. All the while, adding forty-five (45) new single-family units, our total efforts affected an increase in real dollars of more than $20 Million.

Made in United States
Cleveland, OH
06 November 2026

47772396R00029